MONKEYS

Julie Murray

Big Buddy Books

An Imprint of Abdo Publishing
abdobooks.com

abdobooks.com

Published by Abdo Publishing, a division of ABDO, PO Box 398166, Minneapolis, Minnesota 55439.
Copyright © 2020 by Abdo Consulting Group, Inc. International copyrights reserved in all countries.
No part of this book may be reproduced in any form without written permission from the publisher.
Big Buddy Books™ is a trademark and logo of Abdo Publishing.

Printed in the United States of America, North Mankato, Minnesota
052019
092019

THIS BOOK CONTAINS
RECYCLED MATERIALS

Design: Sarah DeYoung, Mighty Media, Inc.
Production: Mighty Media, Inc.
Editor: Liz Salzmann
Cover Photograph: Shutterstock
Interior Photographs: Shutterstock (pp. 5, 6–7, 8, 11, 13, 14, 16–17, 19, 21, 23, 25, 26, 29)

Library of Congress Control Number: 2018939886

Publisher's Cataloging-in-Publication Data
Names: Murray, Julie, author.
Title: Monkeys / by Julie Murray.
Description: Minneapolis, Minnesota : Abdo Publishing, 2020. | Series:
    Animal kingdom | Includes online resources and index.
Identifiers: ISBN 9781532116445 (lib.bdg.) | ISBN 9781532157936 (ebook)
Subjects: LCSH: Monkeys--Juvenile literature. | Monkeys--Behavior--Juvenile
    literature. | Primates--Juvenile literature.
Classification: DDC 599.8--dc23

Contents

PRIMATES

>>>>>>>

Monkeys, gorillas, chimpanzees, bonobos, orangutans, and lemurs are all primates. People are primates too. Primates are some of the smartest animals.

Primates have large brains. They have eyes that look forward. Most primates have flat nails instead of claws.

Many primates have hands with **thumbs**. Thumbs allow them to **grab** and hold things.

Spider monkeys can grab with their hands and feet.

MONKEYS

There are about 200 kinds of monkeys. Most monkeys live in **tropical** forests. Others live on **savannas**.

There are two main groups of monkeys. One group is the Old World monkeys. The other group is the New World monkeys.

This monkey lives in a forest in Costa Rica.

Macaques are Old World monkeys.

Old World monkeys live in **Africa** and **Asia**. Some live in the trees. Others live on the ground. Baboons, macaques, patas monkeys, and proboscis monkeys are Old World monkeys.

New World monkeys live in Mexico, **Central America**, and **South America**. They live in the trees. Spider monkeys, squirrel monkeys, and woolly monkeys are all New World monkeys.

WHAT THEY LOOK LIKE

Monkeys may be different sizes. Old World monkeys are commonly bigger than New World monkeys. Mandrills are some of the largest monkeys. Adults weigh as much as 40 pounds (18 kg).

Pygmy marmosets fit in the palm of a person's hand. Their tails are longer than their bodies!

Marmosets and tamarins are the smallest monkeys. They are New World monkeys. The pygmy marmoset weighs only about five ounces (142 g).

Monkeys have long arms and legs for running and climbing. Many monkeys can **grab** things with their hands and feet. Some New World monkeys can grab things with their tails too.

What Makes Them Different

OLD WORLD MONKEYS	NEW WORLD MONKEYS
Live in Africa and Asia.	Live in Mexico, Central America, and South America.
Live in the trees or on the ground.	Most live in the trees.
Most have 32 teeth.	Most have 36 teeth.
Cannot grab things with their tails.	Some can use their tails to grab things.
Most have long, thin noses.	Most have short, wide noses.

This emperor tamarin has a mustache.

A monkey's fur may be gray, brown, or reddish. Some monkeys have long hair around their faces. They may have **beards** or **mustaches**. Some monkeys have bright colors. Male mandrills have red and blue faces.

TROOPS

> > > > > > >

Monkeys live in groups called troops. Most troops have between five and twenty members. But some troops have as many as 100 monkeys. Troop members eat, play, and sleep together.

Baby monkeys are part of troops.

Troop members often **groom** each other too. They stroke each other's fur. They pick out **insects**, dirt, and seeds. Grooming keeps them clean.

Grooming also helps to build friendships in the troop. Monkeys often groom each other after a fight.

Grooming helps monkeys keep their fur and skin healthy.

EATING

Monkeys spend much of the day looking for food. They eat leaves, fruits, bark, vegetables, seeds, and flowers.

Some monkeys also eat **insects**, spiders, and small birds. Sometimes they share their food with troop members.

Some monkeys eat bananas.

GUARDING AGAINST PREDATORS

Monkeys are food for many predators. They must watch out for lions, leopards, **cheetahs**, **hyenas**, **jackals**, and eagles.

Living in troops helps monkeys stay safe. Monkeys warn each other when predators are near. Troop members hear the warning and run to safety.

Cheetahs hunt monkeys and other animals.

BABY MONKEYS

Some kinds of monkeys have **twins** or **triplets**. But most monkeys have one baby at a time. A newborn monkey holds on to its mother's underside. After a while, the baby monkey rides on its mother's back.

A mother black-capped
squirrel monkey and her baby

Female vervet monkeys stay with their mothers' troops for their entire lives.

Baby monkeys drink their mothers' milk. Later, they begin eating other foods. Young monkeys learn from their mothers. Over time, they learn to find their own food.

Some monkeys stay in their mother's troops. Other monkeys find new troops when they are adults.

SAVING THE MONKEYS

>>>>>>>>

Some monkeys are in danger of dying out. People are cutting down the forests where they live. Some people kill monkeys for their fur. People catch wild monkeys and sell them as pets too.

People are trying to help the monkeys. They have set aside land for them. Monkeys can safely live in these special parks.

The Ubud Monkey Forest in Indonesia houses more than 600 monkeys.

Glossary

Africa—the second-largest continent. Egypt, Libya, and Kenya are in Africa.

Asia—the largest continent. Russia, India, and China are in Asia.

beard—the hair that grows on a man's face. In animals, a growth that looks like a man's beard.

Central America—the southern part of the North American continent. Guatemala, Costa Rica, and Panama are in Central America.

cheetah—a large wild cat that lives in Asia and Africa and is the fastest animal on land.

grab—to take hold of something suddenly.

groom—to clean and care for.

hyena—a wild, doglike animal that lives in Asia and Africa.

insect—a small animal that has six legs and three main parts to its body.

jackal—a wild dog found in Africa and Asia that is like a wolf, but smaller.

mustache—the hair that grows on the upper lip.

savanna—a grassy plain with few or no trees.

South America—the continent surrounded by the Pacific Ocean, the Atlantic Ocean, and the Caribbean Sea. Colombia, Brazil, and Peru are in South America.

thumb—the short, thick finger on the side of the hand.

triplet—one of three babies born to the same mother at the same birth.

tropical—of or relating to parts of the world where temperatures are warm and the air is moist all the time.

twin—one of two babies born to the same mother at the same birth.

Online Resources

Booklinks
NONFICTION NETWORK
FREE! ONLINE NONFICTION RESOURCES

To learn more about monkeys, please visit **abdobooklinks.com** or scan this QR code. These links are routinely monitored and updated to provide the most current information available.

Index